ARI⟨

A BIBLICAL STUDY OF DANCE

"Arise, shine; for your light has come, and the
Glory of the Lord is risen upon you!"

Isaiah 60:1
(New King James Version)

"Get out of bed Jerusalem! Wake up! Put your face in
the sunlight. God's bright glory has risen for you." (Msg)

Cheryl Williams

DEDICATION

I dedicate this book first and foremost to my Heavenly Father, because of Him, I live, move and have my being. I love You because You first loved me. I'm so thankful and grateful for the love You show me daily and I appreciate who You are, all that You are, and all that You do through me. Lord, it is evident that without You, I am nothing, but with You I can do all things through Christ who strengthens me.

To my husband, Jessie, my number one supporter, a man who's loving, understanding, and gives of himself. Honey, thanks for the unconditional love you always give; believing and trusting in me. I love and cherish you forever!

To my children, Tarea, Ericka, and Latrice for your continued love and support. Thanks for bringing joy in my life over the years. You all are precious gifts to me and I love you dearly.

To my Pastors John and Pam Antonucci, of Faith Fellowship World Outreach Ministries Church. Words cannot express how much I appreciate the love and encouragement you give to me and my family. Thanks for walking in Godly leadership.

To my former pastors, the late Bishop Isaiah S. Williams, Jr. and Senior Pastor, Dr. Gloria Y. Williams, of Jesus People Ministries Church International. Thank you for laying the foundation and planting seeds of excellence and discipline; living your lives as great examples to the Body of Christ. I love you to Life!

Lastly, I dedicate this book to my loving mother, Mrs. Ella Lee Williams Chipman, who is now seated in the heavenlies, in the presence of the Lord. I'm so grateful to have had a mother, a widow, a teacher, a single parent and a mentor to many, who sacrificed so much, and by the grace of God raised four children in the fear and admonition of the Lord. You were the epitome of the best mother any person could ever have and I am forever thankful. You are so missed and will always be in my heart. I love you forever!

TABLE OF CONTENTS

Page

ARISE!
(A Word to Encourage)

When you hear the word arise, the first thing comes to mind is to "get up." You may have been in a position (posture) of sitting, lying or kneeling. The Hebrew word for arise is "quwm," which is pronounced "koom." There are several meanings to the word Arise, such as: to rise, awaken, come into being, to move upward, ascend, lift up, raise up again, soar, wake up, spring, and many more. Remember, Jesus arose on the third day! Hallelujah!

Now is the time as dance ministers, we must demonstrate the Glory and power of Almighty God in the earth through our gift, our anointing, that the Lord has entrusted to us. We can no longer be enslaved to complacency and mediocrity in the Kingdom of God. He wants all and nothing less. It all starts with surrender; and in addition, prayer and intercession, humility, obedience to His word, love, and faith.

In this book, you will be given a biblical study of dance in the Kingdom of God. It begins with the history of dance from the Old and New Testaments, priestly garments, worship, choreography, etc. As a minister of dance, our assignment is to prophetically convey the word of God through movement to bring salvation, healing, restoration and deliverance to the nations. Isaiah 61:1 says, *"the Spirit of the Lord is upon me, for he has anointed me to preach good tidings to the poor, he has sent me to heal the brokenhearted, to proclaim liberty to the captives, and the opening of the prison to those who are bound."* As you can see, our work is not finished. Please allow the Lord to continue the good work He has begun in you (Phil. 1:6). Remember, satan comes to steal, kill, and destroy; but Jesus came that we would have life and that more abundantly. Don't allow the enemy to steal your joy, your gift, your anointing, your purpose, your life!

He has called us out of darkness into His marvelous light. Because Jesus is the Light, our light can only shine through Him and without Him, there is no light. The scripture says, *"Arise, shine, for your light has come and the Glory of the Lord is risen upon you." (Isa. 60:1)* I challenge you today as you read this book, begin to seek the Lord; seek His word, seek His heart, and ask Him to give you the revelation on the plan and purpose He has for your life, concerning dance. Beloved, you are destined for greatness in the Kingdom of God, and now is the time to go to the next level and ARISE!

CHAPTER ONE

DANCE IN THE OLD TESTAMENT

The word *dance* appears in various forms (danced, dances, dancing) throughout the Bible. Dance is described as emotional movements of the body – to whirl, spin, leap, jump, extend hands, stamp feet. Dance was an integral part of the celebrations of the ancient Israelites. It was used both in worship in ordinary life and on occasions of triumphant victory and festivity. The first mention of dance as a form of worship in scripture is found in the book of Exodus, when the nation of Israel had just crossed the Red Sea, **"And Miriam the prophetess, the sister of Aaron and Moses, took a timbrel in her hand; and all the women went out after her with timbrels and with dances" (Exod. 15:20).** Miriam led the women with joy and dancing. It was a time of thanksgiving, praise, and celebration. Pharaoh's approaching army would have brought certain death, but God brought victory, faith, and life to his people.

We are exhorted to praise God with "dancing, making melody unto Him with timbrel and lyre" (**Psalms 149:3**), and to "praise Him with timbrel and dance" (**Psalms 150:4**). There are several Hebrew words that concern dancing: **chiwl**, which means to twist or whirl; **machowl**, a round dance; **chagag**, to move in a circle; **pazaz**, to spring; **giyl**, to spin around with violent motion; **karar**, to dance whirl about; **pazaz**, to spring; **shachah**, to depress (press down), only to name a few. The most frequently used root for the word "dance" in the Old Testament is **hul**, which refers to the whirl of the dance and implies highly active movement.

An example is when "David danced before the Lord with all his might." David was overjoyed and wanted to express himself in movement because of the return of the Ark (**2 Sam 6:14**). He entered into the presence of God and was "clamorously foolish" as a result of this victory. Another example of dance celebrated in the Old Testament was, when "David slew Goliath; the women sang one to another in dance" (**I Sam 29:5**). These women were praising God and rejoicing with songs and spontaneous worship. The same applies to this present day. Let's allow our dance forms be an expression in our daily life and also victorious times.

DANCE IN THE OLD TESTAMENT
PRACTICE REVIEW

1. Dance is described as _____movements of the body----to whirl, spin, leap, jump, extend hands, stamp feet.

2. The first mention of dance is found in what scripture?

   _____

3. Write out Psalms 150:4.

   _____

4. Hebrew words for dance.

   machowl means _____
   karar means_____
   giyl means_____
   hul means_____

5. Then David danced before the Lord with all his might; and David was wearing a linen ephod.
   Where is this scripture found? _____

6. Write in your own words what you learned about dance in the Old Testament and how you can relate it to dance in this present day._____

   _____

   _____

CHAPTER TWO

DANCE IN THE NEW TESTAMENT

Dance is also an expression of prayer or worship through body movement. The use of dance for celebration and for praising God is prevalent throughout the Bible.

The first mention of dance in the New Testament is found in the book of Matthew, when Jesus departed the twelve disciples and went into their cities to teach and to preach about the Kingdom. Jesus condemned the attitude of his generation. No matter what he said or did, they took the opposite view. He commented, "they were like children sitting in the marketplaces and calling to their companions, saying: "we played the flute for you, and you did not dance; we mourned to you, and you did not lament," (**Matt. 11:16-17**). This generation was cynical and skeptical because he challenged their comfortable, secure, self-centered lives. So the evidence of the use of dance as an accepted expression of joy (praise and worship) is reflected in Jesus comment.

A few Greek words that refer to dancing are: **chorus**, which means a round dance; **skirtao** means to jump; also **proskuneo** meaning to lay prostrate; and **agalliao** which means to jump for joy.

There was other mention of the word dance in the New Testament that appeared in two contexts: Herod's banquet, when Salome danced for his birthday but ended with disastrous results for the head of John the Baptist (**Read Mark 6:21-22**). Unfortunately, in this example, this dance was expressed with the wrong motive.

The other example was the celebration of the Prodigal Son's return **(Read Luke 15:22-27)**. The New Testament provides few specific references to the word "dance." However, "rejoice" is used throughout the scriptures which is the same; along with other references to dancing.

DANCE IN THE NEW TESTAMENT
PRACTICE REVIEW

1. Where is the first mention of dance in the New Testament?

   _____

2. What happened at Herod's banquet?

   _____

   _____

   _____

   _____

3. What scripture describes the celebration of the Prodigal Son? _____

4. Another word for "dance" in the New Testament is

   _____.

5. Greek words for dance.

   choros means _____
   skirtao means _____
   proskuneo means _____
   agalliao means _____

6. Who was Salome? What did you learn about dance in the New Testament?

   _____

   _____

   _____

CHAPTER THREE

OUR ROLE AS NEW TESTAMENT PRIESTS
PRIESTLY GARMENTS/COLORS

Our Role As New Testament Priests

What is a priest? A priest is a minister; elder; one who presides over things pertaining to God. Our role as New Testaments Priests is to be helps ministers to the one and only High Priest, Jesus Christ. Jesus was a fulfilment of the perfect priesthood. It is our responsibility to help accomplish the vision and the purpose of God, set forth in the Lord's community, the Church. Our task is to help fulfill the vision of the house for worship. As dance ministers, we must seek God's vision and wisdom to lead the people to God through our praise and worship in dance.

We must fit within God's purpose and never think more highly of ourselves than we ought (Rom. 12:3). But we should rejoice in the honor of knowing that we have been called to "arise" in revelation and faith, in purity of heart and motivation, as our brother Aaron, from the tribe of Levi, did long ago, to support the purpose of God and His chosen leaders. It is a high and noble calling that we should never take lightly. Jesus serves as our High Priest in heaven, and appears in God's presence on our behalf.

Priestly Garments

Exod. 28:2 states, "And you shall make holy garments for Aaron, your brother, <u>for glory and for beauty</u>."

Moses was instructed by God that the garments of the priests were to be dignified and beautiful, as precious as the garments of royalty. During this time, Aaron, Moses brother, was the first High Priest and he was to be holy, and to stay away from anything that would define him, because he was the mediator between the Lord and the people. No one was fit to serve in the Temple unless he was wearing the sacred garments (Ex. 39:1). These garments possess certain holiness, powerful enough to sanctify all those who merely came in contact with them. In our expression of present day worship; we too must realize the holiness and power we carry when wearing these priestly garments. They are sanctified (set apart) for the Master's use.

Every garment we wear should be symbolic, from the style to the colors (which will be discussed later). Our garments should always point to Jesus because we are representing Him and not ourselves. Just as priestly garments were important in the Old Testament, so are they just as important in our New Testament Priestly ministry.

We must be very careful not to wear garments that are too tight or too revealing. Be mindful of garments that cling to the body, too shear, or low cut. This will not represent the Holiness of our God. We must be covered in His Holiness; and not only in dress, but in all areas of our life (1 Pet. 1:15-16). See pictures of priestly garments on page 15.

OUR NEW TESTAMENT PRIESTLY GARMENTS

Basic Dance Garments

Every dance minister should wear the basic dance garments underneath your priestly garments (dance dresses, overlays, ephods, tunics, etc.) when preparing for worship. These basic dance garments include: a long sleeve leotard or unitard, tights (footed or footless) and palazzo pants. In doing so, no flesh (legs, thighs, underarms) will be seen and there are no distractions to the people in your congregation or audience. We want to always keep things decent and in order! (1 Cor. 14:40) Remember, we are representing the only High Priest, Jesus Christ, the King of Kings!

Colors

In the Kingdom of God, just as garments are symbolic, so it is with colors. God spoke about colors in many of the scriptures. In studying the book of Exodus, chapter 28 and also chapter 39, you will notice several mention of the colors; blue, purple, gold, and scarlet. We must be sensitive to the Holy Spirit in choosing the colors we wear in our priestly garments. Seek and ask the Lord what garments you should wear and what colors. This is vital because they both should connect with the message in your song and dance. For example: If you are ministering a song about heaven, then blue would be a color to wear because it represents the heavenly realm. Other symbolisms of colors are as follows:

Red – Blood atonement; sacrifice of Christ's blood; remission of sin. Isa. 1:18, Heb. 9:14, Rom. 5:9

Gold – Glory of God; deity; divine nature; kingliness; majesty; the Godhead. Mal. 3:3, 1 Pet. 1:7, Rev. 3:18

Green – Eternal life; restoration; fruitfulness; prosperity; new beginning; new life; freshness; healing; mercy. Ps. 23:2, Isa. 15:6, Rom. 12:12, Luke 23:31.

Blue – Heavenly realm; living waters; the priesthood, authority; revelation knowledge; Holy Spirit. John 6:33, Exod. 27:16.

Turquoise – River of God; sanctification; healing; the life giving flow of the Holy Spirit. Ps. 1:3.

Purple – Royalty; majesty; wealth; power; the name of God; authority; Son-ship; inheritance. Judg. 8:26, Luke 16:19, Rev. 5:10.

White – Purity; holiness; the Bride; righteousness; surrender; peace; light; angels. Dan. 7:9, Matt. 17:2, Mark 9:3, Eph. 5:25, Rev. 4:4.

Black – Righteous judgment; death; evil; punishment; bondage; mourning. John 3:19-20, 2 Pet. 2:17, Jude 13, Rev. 6:5.

Silver – Redemption; strength; revelation; wisdom; grace. Matt. 27:3-8.

Yellow – Light; joy; celebration; glory revealed. Ps. 68:13.

Burgundy – New wine; rejoicing; Blood of Jesus. 1 Pet. 1:2.

Fuschia – Joy; compassion. Ps. 68:13.

Rainbow – Covenant; God's promises. Gen. 9:13, Rev. 4:3.

Orange, Red, Yellow – Consuming fire; Holy Spirit; power and presence of God. Heb. 12:29.

OUR ROLE AS NEW TESTAMENT PRIESTS
PRIESTLY GARMENTS/COLORS
PRACTICE REVIEW

1. What is an elder?

   _____

2. Who was the mediator between the Lord and the people?

   _____
   _____
   _____

3. What are our garments made for and where is the scripture found?

   _____

4. What are some basic dance garments?

   _____
   _____
   _____

5. Who is the High Priest? _____

6. We are representing ourselves when we wear priestly garments. True or False (circle one)

7. We must be covered in His _____;
   and not only in dress, but also in our service, in humility, our thoughts, and all areas of life.

8. Please answer the following:

   a. What color does gold represent?_____
   b. What color does yellow represent? _____
   c. What color docs silver represent?_____

CHAPTER FOUR

CHOREOGRAPHY

Definition

The definition of choreography is to orchestrate; compose; to write down; arrange. The Greek word ***chorea***, which means to dance; the French word ***graphie***, means to write down. In liturgical dance, choreography is a visual picture and interpretation of God's Word. The choreographer can write down the dance movements or directions for the designed, planned steps in advance (Psalms 37:23). Another definition of choreography is the art of arranging a dance routine.

Purpose

The purpose of choreography in the Kingdom is for God's pleasure. It is to express freedom and life, for the dance minister. In 2 Cor. 3:17 the scripture says, "Now the Lord is the Spirit and where the Spirit of the Lord is, there is liberty." Also John 8:32 says, "You shall know the truth and the truth shall make you free." In preparing choreography, each movement should convey the power of the word of God to bring forth victory, celebration and restoration (Exod. 15:20 and Luke 15:25). As dance ministers, the word of God is our standard, our direction, and orchestration for life's steps.

The Role of the Choreographer

The calling of the choreographer in the Kingdom of God is a prophetic gift that should be valued as God has given this person the ability to clearly communicate and visually manifest His glory in the demonstration of spirit and power. The choreographer should be somewhat skillful as well as knowledgeable in the **gift**; well-studied in the written word to rightly divide the word of truth in and through the interpretation of dance (2 Tim. 2:15). She/he should always be in a position of prophetically receiving designed movements from the Holy Spirit.

Different Types of Dance Choreography

In dance choreography there are different types, which include:

Devotional dance – which can be at home or in private. This dance is between you and the Lord. As you may have daily devotion in the word, you can also have daily devotion in your dance; just worshipping the Father in Spirit and in truth (John 4:23-24). The Lord loves it all!

Spontaneous dance – unrehearsed; giving praise, worship or adoration without choreographing moves. This can be expressed, during a worship service, if there is freedom and liberty to dance in your church. But please make sure it is Spirit led; you don't' want to be a distraction or interrupt the flow of the Holy Spirit.

Presentational dance – A group, team, or company of dancers with designed choreographed moves by God.

Congregational dance – Congregational participation. In the Jewish culture, there were celebrations in congregational worship; circle dance, line dances where everyone participated. Make an effort to choose a song selection that your congregation will respond to.

Facial Expressions
Facial expressions are very important when ministering in dance. What is experienced in the spirit should be communicated on your face. When we behold His Glory, we will shine as a reflection of Him!

Movements in Choreography:
    a. Lying prostrate - Shows Humility
    b. Kneeling in sitting position – Submission unto God
    c. Resting on the knees – Yielded to the Father
    d. Standing - Restoration
    e. Rise on your feet – Seeking Him
    f. Jump or leap off the floor – Rejoicing in the Lord

The Master Choreographer
Jesus is our Master Choreographer and in choreographing a dance, we must follow His leading by the Holy Spirit, which comes from prayer, submission, and obedience to His word. When preparing a message through movement, seek to surrender your ALL to God and He will be glorified!

CHOREOGRAPHY
PRACTICE REVIEW

1. The Greek word for choreography is
   _____.

2. What is the definition of choreography?
   _____
   _____

3. What is the purpose of choreography?
   _____
   _____
   _____

4. The calling of the choreographer in the house of the Lord is a
   _____ gift that should be highly
   esteemed.

5. Name the different **types** of dance choreography.
   _____
   _____
   _____
   _____
   _____

6. What are some **dance movements** in choreography?
   _____   _____
   _____   _____
   _____   _____

CHAPTER FIVE

DANCE TYPES
(PRAISE, WORSHIP, WARFARE, PROPHETIC)

PRAISE DANCE
Praise is our offering unto the Lord. Praise is based on covenant. God has commanded us to praise Him. Throughout the scripture, we find God admonishing us to praise. Movements in praise dance can be the lifting up or waving of the hands, jumping, clapping, leaping, etc.

Praise ye the Lord. Sing unto the Lord a new song. Let them praise His name in the dance: let them sing praises unto Him with the timbrel and harp (Ps. 149:3). Praise Him with timbrel and dance: praise Him with the stringed instruments and harp (Ps. 150:4).

WORSHIP DANCE
Worship is God manifesting Himself to us and through us in response to our praise. God initiates worship as we humble ourselves before Him during the worship dance, and God may choose to speak to us prophetically through the prophetic dance, through a prophetic song, or the spoken word. As the word of the Lord is ministered through worship, the anointing will heal, encourage, exhort, correct, or show us what the mind of God is. The Holy Spirit will choreograph worship movements. Usually the movements will be soft, flowing and tender. They will be movements such as: bowing down, kneeling, grasping, and showing love or adoration to Abba Father.

But the hour cometh, and now is, when the true worshippers shall worship the Father in Spirit and in Truth, for the Father seeketh such to worship Him; God is a Spirit; and they that worship Him, must worship Him in Spirit and in Truth (John 4:23-24).

WARFARE DANCE

Praise and worship are powerful weapons of war. As dance is executed, there is a force or "army of soldiers" in the spirit, which make war in the heavenlies. The warfare dance is used to bring deliverance, healing, breakthrough, and the tearing down of any hindrances. The warfare dance is an aggressive dance filled with movements and sounds, such as kicks, punches, stomps, marching, etc. the music will be loud, sharp, dramatic and warlike.

Let the high praises of God be in their mouth, and a two-edged sword in their hand; to execute vengeance upon the heathen, and punishments upon the people; to bind kings with chains, and their nobles with fetters of iron. (Psalms 149:6-8)

PROPHETIC DANCE

Acts 2:17, says, **"And it shall come to pass in the last days, says God, that I will pour out of my Spirit on all flesh; your sons and daughters shall prophesy."** Prophetic dance are movements that are the heartbeat of God revealed to us and through us to accomplish His purposes. Prophecy, however, is the voice of God. It is a message of divine truth revealing God's will. Please understand that you do not have to walk in the office of a prophet to flow prophetically in dance.

Prophetic movements are movements that come from the throne to bring forth divine revelation and truth in the earth (Apostle Dr. Pamela Hardy, 2011). Prophetic dance can be spontaneous or choreographed.

Having then gifts differing according to the grace that is given to us, let us use them: if prophesy, let us prophesy in proportion to our faith. (Rom. 12:6)

DANCE TYPES
(PRAISE/WORSHIP/WARFARE/PROPHETIC
PRACTICE REVIEW

1. Give a scriptural reference to praise dance. Write out the scripture.

   _____

   _____

   _____

2. Name some movements in praise dance.

   _____

3. Give a scriptural reference to worship dance. Write out the scripture.

   _____

   _____

   _____

4. What are some movements in warfare dance?

   _____

   _____

5. In your own words, what is prophetic dance?

   _____

   _____

   _____

6. Give a scriptural reference to prophetic dance. _____

7. Prophetic dance is movements that are the _____ of God revealed to us and through us to accomplish His purposes.

CHAPTER SIX

BIBLICAL FORMS OF WORSHIP

What is worship? The word worship means to bow; to esteem; glory. It also means reverence; to honor; utterly devoted admiration for a person; and lastly, to be full of adoration. Worship is a natural instinct and a basic need for every person. God is the focus of our devotion in both the Old and the New Testament. In Exod. 20:2-3, God says, "I am the Lord your God, you shall have no other gods before me. In Matt. 4:10, Jesus says, "Worship the Lord your God and serve him only." So worship is not only a natural instinct, it's a command from God Himself. God alone is worthy of our devotion, praise and worship. He is our God, our Creator, and we are commanded to praise and worship Him. Psalm 96:9 says, "Worship the Lord in the splendor of his holiness; tremble before him, all the earth." A life of praise and worship fills our deepest needs, and it also brings great joy to God. Zephaniah 3:17 states, "The Lord your God is with you, he is mighty to save. He will take great delight in you, He will quiet you with his love, He will rejoice over you with singing." Worshipping God is a condition of the heart; a willingness to exalt God and submit to His will. True worship is the heart song of a life devoted to Christ.

Worship has to be a genuine expression of who we are, where we are coming from, and where we desire to go. All forms of worship are meaningful. However, the goal is to find and utilize those forms of worship that will draw you closer to the Lord. In the Old and New

Testament, there are many passages and words that indicate various worship forms that are acceptable to God. See below:

- **Kneeling or Bowing** – Psalms 95:6-7, "Come let us bow down in worship, let us kneel before the Lord our Maker; for He is our God and we are the people of His pasture, the flock under His care." Kneeling is definitely an act of humility. You acknowledge the Lord's rule over your heart and you acknowledge His greatness. Kneeling before God is also an act of surrender; surrender to His will, His authority, His love. Daniel continued to kneel before the Lord in full view of Jerusalem even after he found that doing so much would bring him death. He surrendered his very life to the authority of God.

  Philippians 2:9-10 speaks of Jesus when it says, "Therefore God exalted him to the highest place and gave him the name that is above every name, that at the name of Jesus every knee should bow, in heaven and on earth, and under the earth." One day we will all kneel before the Lord in full reverence of His power and excellence. Kneeling can be a powerful form of worship even while reading scripture or just being in the Lord's presence.

  The word "worship" translated in Hebrew means to "bow down." A few scriptural references of bowing were: The wise men bowed and worshipped the baby Jesus (Matt. 2:11)' Many who had plagues and unclean spirits fell down before Jesus and were healed (Mark 3:10 11); The man who was possessed of demons, fell down before Jesus and was delivered (Luke 8:28); Mary fell at Jesus feet and pleaded with him over her brother's death, Lazarus (John 11:32), to name a few.

- **Standing** – The scripture says, "Stand up and praise the Lord your God, who is from everlasting to everlasting. Blessed be your glorious name, and may it be exalted above all blessing and praise." (Nehemiah 9:5). When a dignitary enters the room, you stand. When an athlete makes a great play, you stand. When you are introduced to a person, you stand to greet them. When a bride walks down the aisle, you stand. By standing, you are showing your respect for a position, person, or recognizing great accomplishment. This is all true when worshipping the Lord, because He is worthy of our highest honor. God deserves to be honored in this way as we acknowledge His greatness and Lordship in our lives.

  Some scriptural references of standing are: Moses was standing on holy ground – that is where the Lord is (Exod. 3:5); Samuel stood in the presence of the Lord (I Sam. 12:3); Elijah stood in the presence of the Lord on the mountain (I Kings 19:11); Gabriel stood in the presence of God when proclaiming the birth of Jesus (Luke 1:19).

- **Lifting Hands** – "Lift up your hands in the sanctuary and praise the Lord. May the Lord, the Maker of heaven and earth, bless you from Zion (Psalms 134:2-3). Lifting hands is often associated with the act of surrendering. It is a vulnerable position and demonstrates submissiveness. Lifting hands to the Lord in worship can be used for several purposes:

  1. It shows our reverence of God and acknowledges His presence and power. "Ezra opened the book. All the people could see him because he was standing above them; and as he opened it, the people all stood up. Ezra

2. Praised the Lord, the great God and then all the people answered, Amen, Amen while lifting their hands (Nehemiah 8:5).
3. It is an act of praise and sacrifice. "May my prayer be set before you like incense, may the lifting up of my hands be like the evening sacrifice (Psalms 141:2).
4. It is a physical form of prayer, of entreating for the Lord's mercy. "Hear my cry for mercy as I call to you for help, as I lift up my hands toward your Most Holy Place (Ps. 28:2).

The basis of each of these purposes is surrender. In our recognition of God's role in our lives we lift our hands in surrender. In prayer we surrender to His will. "I will sing praise to you as long as I live, and in your name I will lift up my hands (Ps. 63:4).

- **Singing** – Hebrew Word, Tehillah – "Praise the Lord, how good it is to sing praises to our God, it is pleasant and praise is beautiful (Ps. 147:1). Since singing is so prevalent in our society, it makes sense that singing praises to God is probably the single most common way to worship Him. As with all forms of worship, it is important that the focus always be on God and not on the worship activity. Singing can also become so much a habit that we sometimes forget that we need to be focusing on God. We all come together in worship not to be the same or follow one set path, but to bring glory to the name of our Lord Jesus Christ.

  Some scriptural references on singing are: "Sing to Him, sing praises to Him, tell of all his wonderful acts (I Chron. 16:9); "I will be glad and rejoice in you; I will sing praise to your name, O Most High (Ps. 9:2); The Israelites sang to the water, Spring up O well! (Num. 21:17); In David's Tabernacle, they sang to the Lord (1 Chron. 15:16-27); Jehoshaphat overcame a superior army through prayer and singing (2 Chron. 2:20-22); At the last supper, right before going to Mount of Olives, Jesus and his disciples sang (Mark 14:26); Paul and Silas sang praises to God while in jail, the foundation of the prison was shaken, and their chains were broken (Acts 16:25).

- **Playing Instruments** – "Praise Him with the sounding of the trumpet, praise Him with the harp and lyre, praise Him with tambourine and dancing, praise Him with the stringed instruments and flutes, praise Him with loud cymbals, praise Him with clashing cymbals." (Ps. 150:3-5). God delights in the use of instruments to praise His name. In I Chron. 15:16, we see the use of instruments to enhance our worship singing. David told the leaders of the Levites to appoint their brothers as singers to sing joyful songs accompanied by musical instruments. Even without words, instruments can turn our attention to the Almighty God. In the Greek, playing a musical instrument means to "make melody"; celebrate the divine worship with music.

Other scriptural references on playing instruments: God used a trumpet when calling his people to meet with Him on Mt. Sinai (Exod. 19:16-19); The trumpet was sounded to bring people together (Num. 10:1-8); A trumpet blast, and a shout dropped the walls of Jericho (Josh. 6:20); God will gather his elect with a loud trumpet call (Matt. 24:31); Harps were used by the procession of prophets (1 Sam. 10:5); David played the harp, and Saul found relief from a spirit (1 Sam 16:23); Musical instruments were used in celebration of the ark coming from captivity (2 Sam. 6:5); The harpist playing enabled Elisha to prophesy (2Kings 3:15); Hezekiah wrote of singing with stringed instruments all the days of his life (Isa. 38:20); When the prodigal son came home, they celebrated with music and dancing (Luke 15:25); In heaven, there are harpists playing harps (Rev. 14:2).

- **Clapping** – Hebrew Word, *taqa* – "Oh clap your hands all you people, shout unto God with a voice of triumph (Ps. 47:1). Clapping is used in a various settings to show appreciation to someone for something they have achieved or accomplished. No one has accomplished more than the Lord. Clapping can be in a form of applause. Applause to the Lord is different from applause given at a concert or show. Applauding the Lord can be a way to show our agreement with the truth expressed in a song, it can be a way to show appreciation to the Lord for the way He has touched us in worship, or it can be a way to show our submission to the work of God in our lives. In 2 Kings 11:12, we see applause as a form of commitment, submission, and agreement, "Jehoiada brought out the king's son and put the crown on him, they anointed him, and the people clapped their hands and shouted, 'Long live the King!'" God's word says that "all creation will clap its hands in celebration of Him" (Isa. 55:12).

- Shouting – Hebrew Word, *ruwa* – "Shout aloud and sing for joy, people of Zion, for great is the Holy One of Israel among you." Shouting is a way to show extreme excitement, approval, or praise. We shout for our favorite teams, performers, and even our children. Shouting can also express a firm commitment and determination. Shouting to the Lord can be a way to show both our praise of Him and our

- commitment to His work and His word. We can shout to show our excitement of what God is doing in our lives, or to praise Him for answered prayer.

- Other scriptural references on shouting: The Israelites shouted when God lit the burnt offering, (Lev. 9:24); Gideon's tiny army overcame the Midianites with a trumpet blast and a shout, (Judges 7:20); When the foundation of the temple was laid there was shouting, (Ezra 3:11-13); Blind men shouted to the Lord and received their sight, (Matt. 20:30-34); Jesus victorious entry into Jerusalem was accompanied with shouting, (Matt. 21:9); The Lord's return will be introduced with a shout (1 Thes. 4:16).

- **Silence** – Hebrew Word, *hacah* – "The Lord is in His holy temple, let all the earth keep silence before Him." Our worship does not always require words, sounds or actions. In silence we can hear God speak and in the midst of our worship, silence can help us stop to truly sense God's presence. The simple act of silence before God can also be a demonstration of our faith in Him. Twice in Psalms 62:1-2, David displays this kind of faith, "My soul waits in silence for God only; from Him is my salvation. He only is my rock and my salvation, my stronghold; I shall not be greatly shaken."

- **Giving an Offering** – Hebrew Word, *minchah* – Chron. 16:29 says, "Ascribe to the Lord the glory due His name. Bring an offering and come before Him, worship the Lord in the splendor of his Holiness." Also, in Rom. 12:1, we find, "Therefore, I beseech you brethren by the mercies of God, that you present your bodies as a living sacrifice, holy and acceptable, which is your reasonable service." Giving offerings to God is a way to show our thankfulness for that which he has provided. In giving back to him of the money he has given us, we acknowledge that this money was a blessing from Him. When we are willing to use our strengths, our training, and our experiences for God's work, we show Him our dedication to utilize every part of ourselves for Him. It is specifically the act of giving that glorifies God, not what or how much we give. The sincerity of the worshipper is most important to God. It's not so much about what you give or how much, but that you give with a thankful heart and an attitude of worship.

- **Dance** – Hebrew Word, *mechowlah* – As you learned in Chapter 1, in Exodus 15:20, we find that Miriam led all the Israelite women "with tambourines and dancing," after God delivered them from the Egyptians at the Red Sea. When speaking of the blessings we will receive in heaven, Jesus told the people to "rejoice in that day and leap for joy, because great is your reward in heaven," (Luke 6:23). There are many scriptures that give the use of dance as a way to celebrate the Lord and honor Him. When David's wife, Michal questioned David's unrestrained dancing, David told her he was dancing before the Lord, who appointed him as the leader of Israel. He told her he was willing to look like a fool in order to show his joy in the Lord (2 Sam. 6:21-22 MSG). True praise requires participation of our entire being. It requires heart, mind, emotion, and body.

Additional scriptural references on dance: Dance was used to celebrate military victories, (1 Sam. 18:6); The Lord turns our mourning into dancing, (Ps. 30:11); There is a time to mourn and a time to dance, (Eccl. 3:4); When God restores us, we dance, (Jere. 31:4); Music and dancing was found in the father's house when the prodigal son came home (Luke 15:25); We are exhorted to praise Him in the dance (Ps. 149:3 and Ps. 150:4); David danced before the Lord with all his might when bringing the ark into the tabernacle (2 Sam. 6:14).

BIBLICAL FORMS OF WORSHIP
PRACTICE REVIEW

1. Name 6 biblical forms of worship.

   _____   _____

   _____   _____

   _____   _____

2. In Matt. 4:10, Jesus says, "Worship the Lord your God and
   _____ him only."

3. Write out a scripture pertaining to kneeling.

   _____

   _____

   _____

4. Lifting hands is an act of _____.

5. What is the Hebrew word for singing?

   _____

6. Give a scriptural reference for playing instruments.

   _____

7. Miriam led all the Israelite women with tambourines and

   _____.

8. Is silence a form of worship?   Yes   or   No   (circle one)

9. Clapping is used to show what?

   _____

10. "God is a Spirit, and they that worship Him must worship
    Him in Spirit and in truth."
    Where is this scripture found? _____

CHAPTER SEVEN

STARTING A DANCE MINISTRY

(Questions to Consider)

1. Am I called? How do I know?
   a. Is my life holy and pure before God?
   b. Do I have a heart of surrender?
   c. Am I truly committed to the life of Jesus Christ?
   d. Do I dance into worship, or worship the dance?
   e. Am I ministering to God, before ministering for God?
   f. Do I know what it means to dance prophetically?
   g. How can I be an effective dance leader?

2. Purpose and Vision
   a. What is the purpose of the dance ministry?
   b. What is the vision of the dance ministry?
   c. What is the Pastor's vision?
   d. Does your purpose and vision connect with the vision of the Pastor/Church?

3. Laying a Foundation
   a. Where was dance originated?
   b. Do you know the biblical foundation of dance in both the Old and New Testament?

      c. Are you willing to study to show yourself approved in the Word? (learn Greek/Hebrew language in dance) What about garments, colors, instruments, etc.?

4. Dance Ministry Guidelines
   a. Compose a dance ministry application.
   b. What's the rehearsal schedule?
   c. What ages are included (children, teens, adults?)
   d. Will you commit to attend rehearsals regularly?
   e. How's your attitude toward others?
   f. What is the dress attire for rehearsal?
   g. How does the team prepare to minister?
   h. Do you study the Word during rehearsal?
   i. Do you attend church services regularly?

5. Music Selection
   a. What does the music make you think about?
   b. Does the music support the Word of God?
   c. What type of song is it (praise, worship, prophetic, warfare)?
   d. Describe the message of the song.
   e. Does it inspire others to praise/worship the Lord?
   f. Are the words easily understood?
   g. How danceable is this song for the team?
   h. What message might be delivered through dance that may not be as noticeable through song?

CHAPTER EIGHT

FINAL THOUGHTS

As you can see from the beginning, in the Old Testament, dance was founded on the Word of God. Ephesians 6:14 states "Stand therefore, having our loins gird about with truth." Figuratively speaking, a loin is an expression for the part of the body that involves procreation, bringing forth life. When our loins are filled with God's truth, the ministry of dance will birth life (Sharnell Jackson 2002).

Just as dance started with Miriam, David, and others mentioned previously, it continues to be important in this present age. We also learned that the purpose of dance is to bring glory and honor to God through prophetic movement, and to take the focus off self.

Please also understand that we are not only dance ministers, but we represent the Kingdom of God as New Testament priests where the priestly garments originated. Remember, as we serve God in ministry, we do not wear costumes or outfits; but we wear "holy garments."

Eph. 18:1 says, "may the eyes of your understanding be enlightened; that ye may know what the hope of his calling, and what the riches of the glory of his inheritance in the saints." I encourage you, dance minister, leader, worshipper; as the Lord is leading you to perfect your gift, possibly lead a ministry, or *"Arise"* to your next level of ministry, begin to seek the Lord for direction, seek His heart, trust Him, and He will direct your every step. (Prov. 3:5). Strive to be your best because He gave His best, His Son, Jesus

Christ, Hallelujah! Diligently serve Him with passion and excellence in everything you do; and finally beloved, embrace the love He has for you daily; commit to be obedient and study His word. (2 Tim. 2:15). Don't just be a hearer of the Word, but be a doer of His Word, because His word works! So, Arise son! Arise daughter! and Shine! For your light has come, and the Glory of the Lord is risen upon you!

THE HEART OF A DANCER

*Father, I praise you because I am fearfully and wonderfully made in the image and likeness of your Dear Son; and because of Jesus I have life and that more abundantly. Thank you for loving me with an everlasting love, just the way that I am. I present my mind, body, soul, and spirit as a living sacrifice, holy and acceptable unto You. Lord, I repent of any sin and unrighteousness. Create in me a clean heart, and renew a right spirit within me, so my worship, my dance, is not hindered. Father, it is my desire to worship you in Spirit and in truth. I long to spend more time in your presence; seeking your face, seeking your heart, falling deeper in love with you. Thank you Lord for choosing me and using me as an anointed vessel to dance in the Kingdom of God. I appreciate and protect this prophetic gift that you have entrusted to me. I know that it is not by **my** might, nor by **my** power, but by **your** Spirit in everything I do. Therefore, I commit my life to you totally. I seek first the Kingdom of God and your righteousness, knowing that everything else will be added to me. Father I'm so blessed to know that no weapon formed against me shall ever prosper, and every tongue that rises up against me shall be condemned! Because satan is under my feet, I can dance in total victory! Help me to **not** lean on my own understanding, but acknowledge You in all of my ways. Father, I pray that as I minister in dance, I will demonstrate and exemplify Your Glory and Power in the earth so that lives will be transformed. I love you Lord and I surrender my all to You. I thank you for hearing me when I pray. In Jesus Name!*

Amen

*A*CCOMPLISH - *to achieve; attain; complete*

"So shall My word be that goes forth from My mouth; it shall not return to Me void, but it shall **accomplish** what I please, and it shall prosper in the thing for which I sent it. (Isa. 55:11)

*R*ECEIVE - *to accept; acquire; gain*

"He shall **receive** blessings from the Lord, and righteousness from the God of his salvation. (Ps. 24:5)

*I*NCREASE – *expand; multiply; raise*

"But I will gather the remnant of My flock out of all countries where I have driven them, and bring them back to their folds; and they shall be fruitful and **increase**". (Jere. 23:3)

*S*ERVE – *assist; give; contribute; support*

"**Serve** the Lord with gladness; come before His presence with singing." (Ps. 100:2)

*E*NDURE – *withstand; tolerate; continue*

"Indeed we count them blessed that **endure**. You have heard the perseverance of Job and seen the end intended by the Lord—that the Lord is very compassionate (Jam. 5:11)

Cited Sources:

Maxwell Leadership Bible, Second Edition, New King James Version by Thomas Nelson Publishers,Nashville, TN

Hardy, Pamela Apostle Dr, "Prophetic Dance." June 2011.
www.drpamelahardy.org

Stevenson, Ann, "Restoring the Dance," 1998. Destiny Image Publishers, Inc.

Jackson, Sharnel, "Dance In Its Purpose," 2002.

Smith's Bible Dictionary, Revised Edition, published by Holman Bible Publishers, Nashville, TN

Strong's Exhaustive Concordance of the Bible, Hebrew/Greek Language, by James Strong, S.T.D. Published by Holman Bible Publishers, Nashville, TN

The New Webster's Thesaurus, Donald O. Bolander, M.A., and Jean A. McCormick Vreeland, M.Ed. Lexicon Publications, Inc. Danbury, CT.

NOTES

For additional information about Cheryl Williams Ministries, or to arrange for speaking/teaching or ministry engagements, please contact:

Cheryl Williams

Phone: (239) 368-9945
Fax: (239) 368-9945

email:
cherylwilliamsministries@gmail.com

Coming soon! - "Arise" DVD

Made in the USA
Charleston, SC
22 July 2014